A SOLDIER' S THOUGHTS

Derrick L. Randall

A SOLDIER'S THOUGHTS

ISBN-13: 978-0692239117

ISBN-10: 0692239111

This book is dedicated to my three guardian angels: Agnes Hill Barton, Diane "Cookie" Green, John Washington, Jr. …and those who have shaped my existence. My eyes are watering, but my heart remains full of grace. God has been good to me, and for that, I am eternally grateful.

Derrick '14

CONTENTS

A SOLDIER'S THOUGHTS

A Sacrificial Commitment

Thanks For Everything

For You, My Dear

Staying Grounded

Unheard Bliss

Playing My Position

Two Battles, One War

A Bite To Eat

Not Me, But You

Sweetest Name I Know

Oh, What A Day

It Is What It Is

Heavy Is The Head

I Fall To Stand

Derrick

I came from everything, and I still have much more to gain. You will never hear me say I come from nothing. My upbringing was filled with love where monetary wealth lacked.

The true heart of a man is his family. My roots are grounded in the beliefs of those who raised me. My love for God comes from my grandmother's undying faith in prayer. My love for myself comes from my understanding of my mother's love for me. You see, to her I am worth living for which solidifies me. My love for others comes from my aunts and uncles. The bond they share with one another is contagious. It allows me to search for the same amazement when bonding with my cousins. I am a better friend because I was able to witness through their relationships that love may build bonds, but time sustains them. The understanding of my father's stability and humbleness supports my backbone. I am product of those who love.

Today, I lead my own family, which is another testament to the heart of a man. I learn so much as a husband, and it carries over to me, as a man. My wife's love for me sustains me. My kids love for me gives me the understanding that to someone I mean the world. I am a product of those who love me.

I have learned that life is what you allow God to make it. You see, my story was once different. I found solidification in my story when I recognized the writer of it. In return, I was able to accept understanding over unchanging. My story is similar to others;

but of course, it is different in scenarios and situations. We all struggle. We all laugh. We all love. We all hate. Just in different ways for the most part. I have struggled with telling my story on such a level for a long time. I have always believed the best form of advertisement is yourself. Just today, I came to the realization. My story is not mine to hold on to. I am rewriting a story that has already been written. As much as you are now the reader, I am merely the character in this story. Allow me now to present what has been played out, thus far. Therefore, I must warn you that the last page of this book will not be the story's end. It is funny how the author finishes writing, but the story always continues in our heads. The author ultimately writes the story, but we live it. I am choosing to give insight into my Author's story, as I live it. My hope is that I inspire others to embrace life and conceptualize our biggest obstacle sometime can be ourselves.

**Some May Call Them Poems, I Refer To Them As My Life
Stories…**

<u>Enjoy…</u>

What Is A Thought?... My Understanding of Thought

The pondering of one's mind can be liberating, yet it may suffocate others. The need to know allows every individual the ability to engage in thought. Webster Dictionary (2014) describes thought as the process of cogitation; serious consideration; and/or the power to imagine. That definition may seem pretty loaded, but it is actually a military hummer when we are dealing with a Bradley tank.

Thoughts are more than cogitation, consideration, and imagination. Yes, these are accurate explanatory terms. No disagreement here, yet thoughts are much more. Our whole being is driven by thought. The thought of losing a love one can allow an individual to experience heartache prematurely. The thought of today intoxicates while the reality that tomorrow is today brings about sobriety.

Thought may be our most prominent human ability. A shared thought can open the mind of another or shut the door to others' destiny. A thought is powerful and everlasting.

The complexity in embracing what is a thought is a full circle. To understand thought we must enter into thought. That may sound tricky, but it is not. Think about this, no pun intended, where would we be without thought? Some may reply, "Better off!" Others may report, "Lost!" Either way, there was a moment of thought.

Thought only can be truly explained by those who possess it. Thought is an individual possession. Each individual cogitation, consideration, and imagination is stored within. The privy of defining thought is individualistic. To explain or define it, a look within becomes essential.

I decided to look within one day. To my surprise, I realized thoughts are whispers from beyond. I get lost in my thoughts some days. I submit myself into the joy of these whispers. I can remember a time when my thoughts were screams. Now, the pleasant whisper that is my thoughts comfort me. Subsequently, I am not as concerned with "What is a Thought?" No, I am more concerned with the whisperer.

Happy Weekend!!

The simplicity of life is welcoming. Pain and laughter contributes to this simplicity. It is my experienced belief; to encompass joy, one must be willing to encounter pain.

It amazes me how I am able to find so much time to do the many things I have running in my life presently. Just yesterday, I was expressing to someone this exact sentiment. Then it occurred to me being yourself and walking in your purpose is life's most simplest task.

The weekend is in front of me now, and it holds many unfamiliar and some previously visited adventures. There has always been something about tomorrow that strikes a stirring in me. I am not afraid, nor excited about tomorrow...

Appropriately, I have learned to enjoy the simplicity of today!

Enjoy the weekend!!

<u>Why Does It Really Matter...</u>

Just yesterday, I found myself reflecting on certain situations around me. In the midst of my reflecting, I replied aloud, "Why does it matter?" I startled myself, but I also woke up to my Reality. If I am to take the mindset of nothing matters, what do I care about? If I take the mindset that everything matters, do I care too much?

Now, these questions can be answered many different ways. There is no clear cut diamond here sparkling bright at the bottom of the kitchen sink pipe. Sorry, Honey we will have to chalk this one up as a loss. Besides, the answering of one's questions should be done through one's own process of self-exploration, in my opinion.

Back to the point, sorry; I often drift while I drive...

A reflection is often what I see, but when beneficial it can be what I do not want to see. Reality can play a slick hand of Texas Hold'em. Poker face no let us try no face. If Reality has two Aces, it is not worried about me waiting on the river. Chances are Reality won the pot on the draw.

I am inclined to believe what may not matter to me means a lot to Reality. Consequently, I am sitting across from Reality waiting on the river. In reflection, it matters a lot to me, as well.

Each day the river rises. My Reality is not gambling away the chances to matter.

So, how was my driving...

Do You Feel It...

It is like the gentleness of the wind's cool breeze over your shoulder on a pleasant winter night. It is refreshing as cool water pouring into a tin tub on a hot summer day. It is unseen, yet it is present.

It may summon you in the middle of the night, or in the stillness of this moment. It may startle with defiant certainty, yet it imposes in no certain way.

It moves like lighting, but settles like thunder. It engulfs like starvation, but it sustains the hunger.

It is displayed unexpectedly. It attacks from within. It holds no position, yet it sustains to no end.

Close your eyes. Relax your mind. Tell me do you feel it...

It allows the melody to ease your mind. It makes a no rhythm dancer catch a beat. It finds its way in when there are no more seats.

No need to worry there is not anyone capable of stealing it. For no one knows the place nor time they may feel... SPIRIT!

Nothing Exudes Like...

I have always been of the thought that conformation exudes power. I am not too sure this is not true. Yet today, I encountered an interaction to change my outlook.

Power can be given or accepted. Do not let anyone fool you power cannot be taken. Power taken is not real power. It is accepted control.

Conformation is attainable through the conceivable understanding of standing out front and setting about the evolution of the situations affecting our environment. The essence of understanding this assignment is understanding power is gained more prominently than it is accepted. To make my point transparent, giving someone a compliment is substantially empowering to their self-worth regardless of the recipients' intrinsic acceptance.

My point is this, power only exist through deliverance. If you do not believe it, I do not have it. If you do not give it, I do not have it.

Individually, power is gained through the beliefs of those around us. You see, as cute as I may think I look, it means nothing if no one sustains the thought. This is the equivalent to sticking a hatpin in a bright red balloon.

Gained power is intrinsic. Accepted power is sustainable only when those around you believe it and give it. Furthermore, exuding power is understanding its strength is not sustained by the individual out front, but those who choose to follow.

Power: Revisited

Power can be interrupted in various ways. Recently, I expressed my thoughts on power. In the days that have passed, I was privy to encounter a discussion with some intrinsic thinkers who engaged me to further examine my outlook. In counteraction, I have been led to revisit power.

Where does power originally initiate? In the revealing discussion, I had the privilege of partaking; the overall agreement was from individual belief. Previously, I stated those around us instill power. I stand corrected. Those around us solidify and sustain power, but power first has to be initiated. For example, if I never say or act on anything there is no power for others to gain or give. The question then may be, "Who employs you with power in the first place?" My answer is simple. For all I am, and for all I ever will be. I credit my Whisperer.

Power is what we make it. I am as powerless as I allow. You are as powerless as you allow. We all are as powerful as we believe. I believe I am powerful. I believe you are as well. To believe in each other succors the empowering of all.

My power is your power, and Our Power is Immeasurable!

Finding My Way

I can remember being told, "You will not make it in the army." In retrospect, I am honorably retired from the army. I also can recall, "You do not get it." Presently, I am open to understanding.

My point is this, a point that comes from both experience and heartache, nothing is impossible for God. I appreciate advice. I will even take harsh criticism when needed. I realize learning is done on a daily.

It is my desire to live in my purpose. To walk with purpose is commendable, but to walk in purpose is heavenly. One may say, "What is the difference?"

My reply, "If tomorrow will be today, my purpose for walking has already been fulfilled."

Uncaged Soul

I have not written in awhile. I have been feeling some kind of way. Feelings are common nature. In fathom, I have allowed nature to overpower my will to reach within. Therefore, in a stance to regain my will, I have decided to write.

I really do not know what to tell. Besides, it takes a lot to express yourself through written word. It is the equivalent to reaching within one's soul and delivering the discovered contents while fighting through torment and hope.

Expressing myself is liberating. Liberation is quintessential to my soul. Therefore, I am back. Yes, liberation is mine. I am intent on setting my soul free.

I am going to write my thoughts. Tell of my story. This is my journey. It will live forever. In my journey, I have decided to live outside the formidable rights of tradition, and live within the conceptual spirituality of my soul. Some may not fancy what I write, yet it uncages me.

My writing exhibits my freedom. My freedom is my liberation. Therefore, my soul lives free.

<u>This Lovely Sunday</u>

I told you I was back. It is hard to remain quiet when your soul desires to roam free. For love, I continue. Love is a powerful entity.

Love will lead playboys to commitment. Love will summon the heart of an independent woman into understanding dependence can be just as fulfilling. Love covers unprotected children and misguided fools.

What do I know about love? I know it sustained me when I was filled with doubt. I can testify to love comforting me as I complicated everything around me. With eternal gratitude, I am thankful for love. Love is the apotheosis of all things.

Hold on to love. Give love. Cherish love in everything. When all else is gone, love will remain!

Happy Sunday!

<u>No Sole Proprietorship Here</u>

Confidence can often be interrupted as arrogance. In understanding where I am going and what I desire, I have decided to walk with an Undisputed, Undefeated, No Recipe to be Beat Partner.

Wherever I go, I am confident; I will succeed. Whatever I do, I am positive it will be sustainable. My Partner has it covered.

Arrogant, oh well, I explain it as assured confidence. Without my Partner, I could not win a battle. With my Partner, I am undefeated.

There is nothing wrong with arrogance. Traditionally, arrogance is seen as a negative notion. The truth is arrogance enhances belief in one's self.

I believe in myself. Does that make me arrogant? That is not really important. The importance, for me, is where my confidence lies, in my Partner: Undisputed, Undefeated, No Recipe to be Beat.

Cause & Effect

We all have experienced loss, in some form. It can be as simple as losing a coin that my fall out of our hand when receiving change back after making a purchase. In some cases, it can be as heartbreaking as losing a championship game on a bad call by a referee. Of course, in many circumstances, loss is more identifiable and synonymous with a soul wrenching subtraction from our lives.

I have experienced each of the previously stated examples. Yet in each of those examples, I became more familiar with myself. Am I fond of loss? On the surface, no. As a spiritual being, yes, I am grateful for loss.

Contrary to much belief, loss strengthens one's inner being. There are days loss consume my surface so tightly only my soul can free me. Taking or experiencing a loss is the essence of understanding present and future blessings.

Loss does not defeat one's soul. One's soul is enriched through loss. Losing is not easy, yet dying is internal. Copiously, to truly live, loss must be encountered to sustain winning.

<u>Chasing Time</u>

The unexpected things often catch our attention. The expected things are often overlooked. For example, I was sitting in a room today waiting for a meeting to start. Unexpectedly, I stated to the person sitting next to me, "Wow, the ticking of that clock is loud." We agreed on it and moved on. Eventually, the meeting started.

In a sense of expectation, we all know time is moving. The misplaced pleasure in this expectation is we do not hear it. Time moves in many different facets, but have you ever noticed once time is heard everything seems to slow down? In comparison, as long as time is unheard, we seem to be racing against it.

Listen...do you hear the clock ticking? Probably not, because you are currently racing against it...Unexpectedly, stop and listen. In that moment, when you find the clock's ticking to be loud ask yourself, "Why am I running when the pleasure is in listening?"

<u>Go Get It</u>

In the past, I have made situations work for me due to the circumstances surrounding me at the time. In hindsight, most of those situations were not substantially beneficial to me. For example, I can remember working day in and night out to further progress the foundation of something I had neither care nor drive for. You know, getting by to provide. I am not naive. I understand, in most circumstances, that is the way of the world.

Well, those days are long gone. I gave all I had to sustain an ungrateful recipient. My love and passion lives within myself. The best recipient of these attributes is myself. The struggle is over. The fight within has been revealed. If I gave so willing to the ungrateful, why should I not be openly engaging all my power in myself.

The choice is ours. The dilemma is obvious. The answer is tucked within. Reach in and find it. The burden becomes lighter when we release the weight of giving to the ungrateful recipient.

<u>Tracing My Footsteps</u>

I can remember when life was as carefree as a soaring eagle, and the concept of time was as innocent as my mind. I was merely seven years old. My days were filled with love and care. My grandmother was my best friend, and my playmates consisted of my fellow peers in my community… the simplicity of childhood.

I can recall becoming a teenager and feeling myself. I ventured outside of the carefree and innocence of my childhood. I evolved into a know-it-all with all the wrong answers. Yet, I was a sheltered young boy playing the role of an in-the-know teenage man. Yes, I am aware today, it is contradictory. Teenage and man are not synonymous in comparison. Nevertheless, my plight was to prove the comparison was valid… the complexity of adolescents.

I now reflect on those experiences. As resounding as thunder, those experiences resonate in my soul. I embrace the good and bad roads on my journey. The roads have been mine to travel. I was once asked, "If you could do it all over, what would you change?" Outwardly, in that moment, I may have replied, "There is a lot I would change." Yet in the present, I realize in becoming a man you have to fall along the way. Would I do it all over again? Yes, and I would not change a thing.

The gift of my childhood reverberates in my love for life and others. The complexity of my adolescent years exposes my growth in my journey. The sum of both exemplifies my joy in becoming a man.

<u>No Textbook Needed</u>

I have accomplished many achievements in my life. I also have been unfortunate enough to accomplish some irreplaceable mistakes. I have traveled the world and experienced things I never dreamed I would grace the pleasure of doing. I also have experienced unforgettable moments of embarrassment, do to my actions, when traveling and experiencing these pleasures.

For many years, I allowed the latter in each sentence above to structure my being. The reward from which, I soaked in misery. The accomplishment was lost, and the lesson was overlooked. Living will not always accommodate each participant, yet there is something to be learned everyday.

The beauty in accomplishing something is understanding the experience along the way. Experiencing embarrassment and making mistakes may be a part of the lesson. It does not define me as an individual. It defines the experience.

I define me. My mistakes are my misfortunes. My embarrassing moments are a reflection of my actions. My accomplishments are my achievements. My imperfections are my perfections. In accepting these flaws and attributes, I willingly accept life's lessons.

Accomplishments are well learned lessons. Therefore, embarrassing moments and mistakes are my teachers.

Experiencing Hindsight

Reflection is the passageway into the soul. What happens today is essential in understanding the days I have yet the pleasure of witnessing. My present holds a purpose that solidifies my future.

In understanding my grandmother's Saturday night ritual of cooking Sunday dinner and singing "Pass Me Not, O' Gentle Savior", I am able to sustain based on faith. In encompassing my mother's unbreakable love for me, I am able to comprehend the unwavering axiom of unconditional love. In embracing my wife's pleasure for the simple things of which includes me, I am able to submit to the simplicity of equivalence.

In some situations, reflection can be insightful. In other circumstances, reflection can be sorrowful. Yet, reflection is warranted. Without reflection, there is no basis for my being. With reflection, there is me.

09Feb2005: A Heart With A Different Hue

I can feel IT today, yet I experienced IT long ago. IT resonates in my stride. IT filters through my pours. IT calls me when no one else is listening. IT tells me the reasoning for IT.

The day was gloomy and subtle. The place was not known to many. The time was not relevant. The purpose was fulfilled.

IT has no need to be explained. IT is what IT is...

I can hear IT like a melody. I can catch IT like the beat. All shucks now, watch my feet. Gracefully, I move in harmonious rhythm. Never again will I dance alone. IT plays a mean tune. My leg glides with effortless sway. A leg, which is wounded but has been reshaped like the potter's clay.

IT owns my soul, but IT denies my torments pay. IT hovers over me, yet IT guides my way.

IT is the shift. IT is the end and the beginning. IT is mine. I may not address IT. I may suppress IT, but IT is what IT is...

Intrinsic Triumph...yes...that is **IT!**

*WO*MA**N**

Am I more prominent than her? Am I more purposeful than she? Are we equals, or am I a King? Do I really hold it down, or am I simply a self-professed slave owner? These questions are those of the man. You know him. We all proclaim him with our chest buffed out, but can we find him when she finds doubt? Yes, he asks the questions, but the answers are frequently answered and approved by the WOMAN!

She is prominent. She is full of purpose. Equals, definitely, the title of King does not suit her. She reflects an angelic Queen. She totes the responsibility, and allows the master to bask in his self-professed title. She has no questions. You know her. She holds her head high, and we can find her when we are barely getting by. She asks no questions, but she answers and completes the MAN!

The "N" Files

Knowledge can come at the least expected times. In conversation last night, I had the privilege of taking in a profound statement in a very diverse conversation and setting. The dialogue, which could holds its own amongst the most seasoned intellectuals, allowed me, a participant, to witness the indescribable passion that lies within all of us.

The direction and the basis of the dialogue in last night's conservation is not less important today. It stills resonates with me this morning. The passion I witnessed explained two things to me. One, the understanding and love within ourselves when projected unrestricted can transcend the minds of those listening. Two, Passion leads and sustains nations. In the simple aspect of conversation, passion evokes involvement. Granted this involvement can be internal or unwarranted, either way the listener's involvement is evoked.

I have repeatedly said, "Learning is done daily," The beauty of this is experiencing and enjoying the process. The passion from last night's conversation leads me to knowledge. The knowledge being no matter the environment or setting passion evokes the listener. I must point out the setting was not unpleasant, but I will acknowledge it was a pleasant unfamiliarity.

Earlier, I mentioned being privy to a profound statement. I will not commit the unmistakable injustice of not sharing this jewel. Before doing so, I would like to express my sincere and internal appreciation to the open-minded, thought-driven, and self-grounded young lady who blessed me with this statement. Your passion has strengthened my drive. Thank you... without further undo...the statement was so simply stated, as if it resonated in her mind like the concept of there being an end, so there must also be a start. In a moment of self-lost, *(that moment when the listener is present, yet she, as the speaker, was lost in the realization of her understanding)*, she simply asked, **"How can I operate in a society which was founded upon the enslavement of me?"**...

Ain't Going To Worry Me

The beauty of just being. The feel of uninterrupted possibilities. The concept of nothing expected.

Not going to worry me. Taking it light. No time to entertain foolishness. Get lost with the dookie squash.

Mind is relaxed. Heart and soul clear. Make sure you do not call me now. I cannot hear.

What you say, "What are you getting ready for..."

Like I said, "I cannot hear."

But for future reference and no abrupt interruptions, I am ready to do nothing.

In all pleasantries, it would behoove you to find your own tranquility of nothing, or simple put your own something.

<u>Warming Grace</u>

he opened his eyes. The view had become obstructed. he longed for rescue. No one was near. Silence engulfed him, but fear was not present.

he calmly stated, "If Your Will is to be done, I am privileged to be a part of it." The reply came briskly like a purple feather blowing in the mid morning breeze. He replied, "I got you!"

Calmness settled over his soul. A joy rested in his heart. In the middle of nowhere and lost in war, he had peace.

An tragic event. A saved soul. A restored understanding. An unforgiving Partner. A miracle in Baghdad; no, an encounter with God.

In his heart, he is free. In his soul, he is liberated. In God, he trusts. For no other reason than **He** saved me.

Believe Them

Obliviously, I believe lessons are learned each day. Paying attention and catching these lessons/blessings becomes the withstanding task. Not every lesson/blessing may be taste worthy.

In many cases, it is the opposite. In other circumstances, those closest to you are sheep just in wolves' clothing. For example, the lesson in finding out who someone truly is may not reflect who you thought they truly were.

In contrast, it is still a blessing. The nasty taste left in your mouth signifies it is bad. A notification of it may not be appetizing.

Now, let us practice. I am your friend. Allow me to show you who I truly am. If you assume, I am who you think I am, do not be surprised when the inside of your mouth taste like spoil spam.

The taste is familiar, yet it is unpleasant. Conceptually, it should be spit out. Nasty is nasty, right...

<u>Yesterday's Blessing</u>

I have shared many days amongst the living. Yet, I chose not to live. I have slept many nights besides the sleeping. Yet, there was no rest to give.

A tormented mind leads to a weary soul, similar to a misguided child becoming a haunted man. A different journey, but the same experienced road.

I did not live because I was afraid to die. I did not sleep because I found rest intrusive. The concept of peace eluded me. The misery of uncertainty consumed me.

Presently, living comes easy, a dress rehearsal to forever. Currently, sleep comes in the pleasantry of calmness. Graciously, rest is given through the reminder I will one day fly forever.

Appropriately, I have experienced yesterday, so I can live today.

<u>Unexpected Gift</u>

I have heard, "You never know what life may bring." I have always conceptually taken this statement to be negative. I know right, a negative mindset is a dead mindset.

Unbeknownst to my inaccurate conceptual mistaking, the pleasure comes in my exemption of knowing. Sitting here now, I am enjoying the experience of not knowing how this may finish. There is a sense of excitement in being able to experience the unknown.

As an understanding of my newfound conceptual stance, I am convicted to help life in its distribution of the unknown. Theoretically, whatever life brings is a welcoming surprise. For without it, there is no gift.

<u>A Sacrificial Commitment</u>

There is no personal vendetta directive in what I write. I write from my personal understanding and experiences. I write to share my thoughts in hope that others will be able to relate or experience reflection.

I write to free my soul of the wonders of my mind. I write to fill the emptiness of my outward being. I write to see how far my imagination can go.

I write. I write. I write...

I do not write to garner outside approval. I do not write to confuse. I do not write to ridicule.

Let the words carry your mind. Allow the paragraphs to float through your soul. Become encompassed by the message.

I write. I write. I write...

I write my personal thoughts, so others can freely embrace their own.

<u>Thanks For Everything</u>

His presence is humble. His approach is irreplaceable. He tells not much, yet he has the last say so.

He walks with confidence. He holds his own. He leads with no need of recognition.

He embraces his responsibility with ease. He exemplifies a reflective future. He is a hero.

He is not practical or superficial. He is genuine.

He gives his all without hesitation. He loves under no limitation.

He is a Father.

<u>For You, My Dear</u>

Your approach may be stern, yet your love is gentle. As quick as your voice may rise, your heart is just as subtle. You may frown, but your soul will not buckle.

A simple grilled cheese before school. A quiet I love you at night. The certainty of happiness transcended through your smile.

The title is yours and yours alone. A woman is a beautiful creation, but a Mother stands alone!

<u>Staying Grounded</u>

Life is so unexpected. The joy of one moment can be triumph by the sadness of events that take place in the next hour. In those spans of time, I have chosen to relay my burden to internal truth.

In no way, consider this to be an easy task. It takes intrinsic commitment and soul found strength. The sun comes up, but it also sets. It is simply witnessed, but the preparation of the task is unknown.

Nothing is easily accomplished, in retrospect. It is just transparent. In all transparency, what good is logic if it tells no truth...

Unheard Bliss

The heaviness of pain can crumble. The softness of hurt can inflict incompatible heartache.

Silence soothes...

At a moments notice, hope can be transcended into doubt. In a twenty-four hour time span, today is missed.

Silence soothes...

Pain, hurt, hope, and doubt are essential, yet silence is quintessential. Close your eyes and hear nothing...

Soothing... right...

Silence moves with purpose. Grab hold of it, and hold on tight. Peace comes in quiet understanding. It engulfs the soul and soothes the mind.

Open your eyes and reflect...

Soothing... right...

<u>Playing My Position</u>

Positive is a state of mind. Where I position my outlook will undeniably set up my outcome. In thinking positive, I experience such.

Negative has a position to play, as well. Just be careful because this joker is hell. Yep, negativity gets down through there.

I take the bad with the good. I walk with positivity putting negativity on the run. Sprinting has never been my thing. I always seem to get tired.

While when walking, I breathe just fine. Yes...yes...

Positivity is divine.

Two Battles, One War

To understand what I write, I must first believe it. In no way, am I saying, "Everyone should believe it, as well." However, we all believe something.

My belief is mine. Your belief is your own. There is reasoning for both.

Setting a standardized reality for all is intrusive to individual belief. For example, beauty is in the eye of the beholder. Formidably, if you understand what I see as beauty everything is fine. Unfortunately, if my interpretation of beauty is dismissed the standardization of beauty has been formulated.

Living within my own belief allows me individuality. Living within standardized individuality constraints my reality, if I am an individual; why should I not control my individualism?

Internally, I know what I know. Outwardly, I process everything else. It is the dynamic of two matrices. Recognition of both is essential. For without it, my writing is unwarranted.

No Laughing Matter

I laugh at things that are not funny. I cry about things that should make me happy. Blessings usually do not come in pleasant situations.

I laugh at things that do not matter. Yet, I cry when things matter most. Pleasantries are reflected after conceptualizing blessings.

In explaining my dilemma, I am opening up my conscience to others. "What is the point..." one may ask.

My point is simple. I understand my happiness is not mine to control. It is for God to give.

I Am Drinking Truth & Red Bull

The harmony of unity is everlasting. So much so as a spiritual being, I am constantly trying to echo the melody. On vacation recently, I experienced such harmony.

I will not convey the location of my vacation, but I will share I experienced, "One Love". In observing my surroundings on this tranquility-filled break, I witnessed the understanding of self in one's own environment.

To be in touch with unity, I must encompass soul purpose. I cannot contribute to the revolution if I am not in touch with my own self-evolution... harmoniously conveying ..."One Love"

<u>No One, No Cry</u>

While on a transcending break, I experienced tranquility and bliss. The delivery of such a treat was served on a sun setting silver tray.

The silver tray I am referring to is rich in love. It is solidified in the resistance of time's ever present adversities. The silver tray welcomes with full authenticity, and it pleases to no end.

I have a silver tray that I call my own. Yet, the silver tray I experienced engrossed my heart and stirred my soul. It caressed my being. It welcomed me home.

I would like to thank the sun setting silver tray for endearing me to the following revelation. Polishing a silver tray is much like harmonious unity. Resonates of both occurrences reflect the shinning we all have within.

<u>Setting With The Sun</u>

I have always assumed and heard thunder comes before lightning. I interpreted this to mean when I hear thunder lightning is sure to follow. In harmonious reflection, I misinterpreted the true sentiment of the statement. For example, tomorrow comes after today, but that does not mean tomorrow will come.

Therefore, thunder may be heard, but lightning may not be seen. The presence of thunder initiates the existence of lightning, yet it does not guarantee lightning's presence. Thunder's existence reflects individuality. Lightning's presence solidifies unity.

Understanding, for me, is the undertaking of collective unity. Sitting here now staring into the sunset, I am united with love.

Thunder may take place without the post occurrence of lightning. However, both occurrences are preambles to a storm. Yet, they are unified in perspective.

Unity transcends hope when there is no peace, and Love withstands the storm.

A Bite To Eat

I observed a profound display of blind unity today. I am still feeling the effects of this lasting undertaking as I write now. A memory holds an uninterrupted place in one's mind.

I witnessed a mature and older woman sitting at a table enjoying her dinner. After awhile, two younger women who inquired to sit with her approached her. She openly welcomed them. I must admit I had been watching the mature and older woman on previous nights while dining. She always sat alone, and she seemed to be standoffish. I know right, how judgmental could I be?

Anyhow, once the younger women sat down with the mature and older woman, the united group thoroughly began to enjoy their dinner and each other's conversation.

I mentioned earlier that I observed the mature and older woman on previous occasions sitting alone. She was comfortable in those moments. However, once the young women joined her I witnessed the profound significance of unity.

My observation led me to this understanding when alone contentment is functional. Observantly, when there is unity peace is shared.

<u>Not Me, But You</u>

Everything I am and ever will be is because of You.

Am I always worthy? Certainly not.

I feel Your warmth when my being submits to the cold.

Your grace embraces my soul.

I have experienced many things. All because You saw fit.

Some were bad, but Your love restored good.

I hear You in the loudness of the day. I hear You in the quietness of

the night.

I humbly follow Your light.

I find comfort in Your word. I seek peace in Your presence.

I depend on You. I Love You. Yes, You.

For everything I am and ever will be is because of You!

My Rock, My Provider, My Jesus, My God... Thank You!!

Sweetest Name I Know

My desire is to fulfill my purpose.

My hope is to inspire others.

My soul burns to glorify my Savior's name.

I live in fulfillment.

I live in hope.

I live in my Savior's will.

I am whole.

I am forever waiting.

I am my Savior's child.

He is my everything.

He is love.

Anybody know, Jesus...

<u>Oh, What A Day</u>

If I could give my all, I would.

If I had to, it is done.

Just to hold the space.

To look eye to eye.

To take in a breathe.

Just for the embrace.

Oh, what a feeling.

Oh, how I want to see You.

Just to look upon Your face.

<u>It Is What It Is</u>

I have found trouble to be clever. It does not always follow me, but it will go where I lead. I realize with profound conceptualization that I am accountable for each situation I encounter. The blame is mine. The situation is what it is.

Now in understanding this, I have two choices. I can one, pretend as if this understanding does not exist. Or I can two, high five my reality. The situation is what it is.

The dilemma in this understanding becomes in realizing I may have to accept blame. In all simplicity, it is less taxing to distribute blame outwardly than inwardly. However, in all complexity, auditing someone else for my blame is fraudulent. The situation is what it is.

I do not want it. Nobody else wants it. Yet, it belongs to someone.

Outwitting trouble is lucrative. The profit comes in me accepting my own blame.

<u>Heavy Is The Head...</u>

I fight with having the answer. I struggle with making the right choice. I agonize if I am even in touch with my surroundings.

Twelve rounds later, nothing has changed. The question is the same. The struggle is still apparent. The right choice has to be made. Agony is untouchable. My surroundings are within reach.

Do I really know something? Alternatively, do I know nothing?

My fight, my struggle, and my agony are something. For nothing is neither better nor worse than something.

Nothing is just nothing.

<u>I Fall To Stand</u>

I am accountable to lead. It is written. I have a responsibility. It is mine to understand.

Can I stand before others and proclaim my title? Am I worthy to withstand my duty? Do I comprehend my worth?

I know my position. Time to encompass the feat. I am willing to stand tall and welcome the truth.

No, it is not easy. At times, I may fall. Call me what you may. Yes, I will stumble along the way.

The honor I hold is bestowed. The responsibility I referenced previously is a blueprinted demand. It is mine to understand. Boys learn hard lessons to one day solidify the title of Man.

Lock your doors, but open your heart to the Lord

It is hard, but it is fair

1Luv JWJ

Dad…Out

www.ingramcontent.com/pod-product-compliance
Lightning Source LLC
Chambersburg PA
CBHW031530040426
42445CB00009B/460